How to Rank in YouTube

JAMES GREEN

Copyright © 2014 James Green

All rights reserved.

ISBN: 1497314968
ISBN-13: 978-1497314962

CONTENTS

	Introduction	1
	Who is this book for?	4
	Why use YouTube?	6
	What will I need?	8
1	Videos that get noticed	10
2	Keyword Research	14
	Your video filename	16
	Your Title	17
	Your Description	21
	Using Tags	24
3	Engaging your viewers	26
	Using Annotations	29
	Making your videos 'clickable'	32
	'In-Video' Captions	35
4	Supercharging your traffic	37
	Begin Close to Home	39
	Getting Backlinks	41
	Outsourcing	44
	Getting more Views	46
	PAD Links	49

		Social Bookmarking	51
5	Repurposing your Videos		52
		YouTube is not the only fruit	54
		Repurposing Ritual	56
	Summary		58
	Appendix – Equipment and Resources		60
	Other Books in this series		62

INTRODUCTION

For internet marketers and online businesses alike, the internet landscape is constantly shifting and it can sometimes be difficult to keep up in order to make a success of yourself online.

What worked yesterday doesn't necessarily work today. So we need to find new avenues and new approaches in order to remain successful.

Following the Google Panda and Penguin algorithms (and more recently, Hummingbird), there is a concerted effort to weed out the 'spammy' sites from the internet and the less than savory individuals who were out to make a fast buck.

But along the way, innocent individuals have also been hit for not playing strictly by the rules. And that included me just a few years ago.

So we now need to adapt and learn new ways of getting traffic and income and be more creative in our sources and methods of driving traffic and sales.

One of the most surprising results of my research was just how incredibly powerful two sites in particular were and which very few people were really tapping into to their full extent: *Amazon* and

YouTube.

Both of these have certain very important things in common that make them extremely effective as marketing tools.

They are both what are known as 'self-searching' sites i.e. individuals use them as search engines in their own right. And many millions of individuals do just that: they use *YouTube* to carry out all of their video-related searches in preference to using a generic search engine like Google.

But what makes them especially powerful is that they are also 'self-ranking' i.e. Google also loves to include them in their own search results (hmm, could this possibly be because they own *YouTube*?). And not only Google, but the other search engines too.

For *YouTube*, this gives it a tremendous 'double-whammy' effect. If you simply have a video presence on *YouTube*, then by following some simple rules that I'll show you, they simply cannot fail to show up - either on *YouTube* itself or on any other search engine, particularly Google!

So, by hook or by crook, a searcher simply can't fail to end up on *YouTube* for the vast majority of searches, whether they're looking for a recipe, learning a language or trying to fix their PC.

But what makes *YouTube* super-exciting is that it operates a little like Google used to 10-15 years ago: believe it or not *YouTube* is nowhere near as saturated as traditional websites and many of the strategies you used to employ with Google to get high rankings still works here!

Think about it: every Tom, Dick and Harry has one or more websites nowadays, but by comparison relatively few businesses and individually use *YouTube* in anger in order to earn an income. And those that do will certainly not be harnessing it as powerfully and as effectively as you will be, using the methods in this book.

A lot of people are put off making *YouTube* videos as they believe it will be too hard or that they will need lots of expensive equipment, neither of which are true!

And believe it or not, you will still, even now, be coming to this technology at pretty much the ground floor!

I'll show you how, with very quick and simple techniques, you can get thousands of views of your videos. Not only that, but I'll also show you how you can link these videos to your existing blog, Facebook and Twitter accounts so that they reinforce each other to supercharge all your traffic.

And as I'll demonstrate, you really don't need any fancy tools to get started making videos straightaway. In fact, you don't even need to stand in front of a camera if the idea of that scares the pants off you! You simply need some simple free screen-casting software and a microphone.

What I won't be doing is filling up the book with lots of superfluous tactics that have little or no impact on your rankings. So if they're absent, the chances are good that they simply aren't effective so you can safely ignore them. Time is of the essence so I'm only showing you the methods that give you the biggest 'bang for your buck', that produce strong, tangible results that you'll be able to see the effects of now and going forward.

I'll also be showing you how to outsource some of your marketing efforts to drive a ton of traffic to your videos; as well as the specific areas where you should be using outsourcers... and where you really shouldn't!

Get it right and you can be enjoying residual income from a very small number of videos for many years to come, without ever needing to update them!

If you already have videos out there, follow through the steps in this book and check off each point as you go. The methods are laid out in logical steps so you should be able to follow the strategies through from one chapter to the next.

So let's get started!

WHO IS THIS BOOK FOR?

I have purposefully pitched this book at people who already know a little about how to use YouTube and who may even have one or two videos but simply need to know how to maximize their traffic and views.

I'm not expecting you to know *YouTube* inside out and in fact I will be showing you how to use the main features in *YouTube*, using screenshots along the way to help you. But I won't be too prescriptive about how to make your videos either - that part is very much up to you.

I will however be giving you lots of tips as well as the pitfalls to watch out for when making videos in my "Videos that get noticed" section.

Most people are able to use *YouTube* and, with all the software tools available on the internet, just about anyone can make a video. But surprisingly few people use all of the features of *YouTube* once a video has been uploaded to get it ranking well. They simply fail to take to those extra final steps that make all the difference.

Most simply post a video up and then sit and hope the visitors will arrive in their droves. That way will lead to disappointment!

In order to avoid putting up lots of boring screenshots on the basics of *YouTube* I'm going to assume you:

- know how set up a *YouTube* account;

- know how to do basic keyword research using the Google AdWords Keyword Planner tool (although I will touch on how to do this);

- have a modicum of technical expertise!

I'm also assuming you have an idea about how to create your own videos or have already done so, so I won't be boring you with pages and pages of video production techniques and how to use all the various video editing packages.

This is a very personal choice and there really are countless ways of producing videos, many of them free, some of them very expensive. But you can see the equipment I use and recommend in the Appendix at the back of this book.

This book is very much more about how you can get those all-important viewers, keep them coming back and how to go about putting yourself firmly on page one for your chosen set of keywords.

So whether you're using screen-casting techniques or a face-to-camera method, both are equally valid - you simply choose which is the most appropriate for the niche you are in.

But as I'll keep saying throughout, make sure the information you're putting out there is valuable and engaging as, no matter how many views you get, it's the quality that keeps them coming back for more!

WHY USE YOUTUBE?

At the time of writing, it's official - YouTube is the second most popular search engine in the world after Google. And just to repeat what I said earlier, it really is used as a search engine in its own right!

There are now over 1 billion viewers of *YouTube* across the globe, and it just keeps growing. Over 4 billion *YouTube* videos are viewed each day and in 2012, *YouTube* had well over a trillion views!

A leading internet research company, *Comscore*, found that visitors typically spend 7 ½ times longer watching *YouTube* videos than their nearest competitor, Yahoo and with nearly 3 times more viewers! In fact, they found that 99% of all searchers on Google looking for videos went straight to *YouTube*.

Which site do YOU think of first if you want to watch a video (non-pornographic, I mean!)? Yes, *YouTube*! And the viewers are yours for the taking.

In fact, try it now. Go to Google and type in "how to" [fill in the blank, e.g. make pancakes] followed by the word "video". How may *YouTube* results do you see in the top 5 results? In fact, take out the word "video" - chances are there will still be a scattering of *YouTube* results on page one!

Videos appeal to the masses and provide a tremendous 'instant fix', particularly so now, with literacy and concentration levels at an all-time low; couple this with a need to get to information quickly, people will always turn to videos over text!

And just by following the simple strategies outlined in this book and you'll be ranking in no time for whatever particular niche you are in.

What also makes *YouTube* so powerful is what I call its 'stickiness': there are very few sites that people will linger on outside of *YouTube*, and this is all down to its video content. Visitors may spend hours sitting in this one single site. So you can see why Google returns *YouTube* results at the top of its rankings for just about any search phrase!

Combine this with the *self-ranking* as well as *self-searching* capabilities of *YouTube* I mentioned earlier, then you can see why I firmly believe that this is really where you need to start seriously thinking about concentrating your marketing efforts.

There's an old adage that goes something like, 'if it sounds too good to be true, then it probably is'. Sorry to disappoint you all but this expression simply does not apply to *YouTube* marketing and I can't see it changing, at least for the foreseeable future!

Here is where you need to start concentrating your efforts. Make a good set of videos and use the tactics in this book and you'll be seeing the fruits of your labors for many years to come.

WHAT WILL I NEED?

First of all, don't be scared.

Unless you're planning on doing a big stage production, then you won't need expensive cameras, lighting, green screens, etc. to make videos that will attract thousands of viewers.

If you're planning on putting yourself on camera then you can use anything from a home movie camera to a mobile phone or a tablet. If you do want to go down this route, then there's plenty of good software you can use, such as *iMovie*, *VideoEdit* or *ReelDirector*.

The videos I tend to make are simply 'how-to' instructional tutorials, so I'll be focusing on the 'screencast' video techniques, where you're basically filming your own computer screen.

(If you're interested in the exact equipment I use then see the Appendix at the back of the book, where I'll also give you a link to my own scripting document on my website that I use for producing my own scripts). If you are new to this, then a detailed script is highly recommended. This document also includes an 'action' column, which is a cue for you to do something during this part of your speech.

I'm assuming you all have your own ways of capturing your videos. For the screen-casting technique I simply use:

- A microphone;

- Camtasia Studio screencast software (but I have also used the free CamStudio software in conjunction with Windows Movie Maker, which still produces very effective results).

...and that's it!

The point is, it's really not about the lighting or the 3D stereo sound (unless that's what you're promoting!). It's really all about the quality of the content in the videos themselves and that you are providing something of value to your viewers. In fact, many of the most popular videos currently on *YouTube* were simply taken on a mobile phone!

Whichever method you use, be natural, keep it engaging and make sure that what you're producing is what people want to watch!

1 VIDEOS THAT GET NOTICED

There's a whole bunch of ways to make videos and with all the latest technologies at your disposal it's now pretty easy to put a video together.

Many videos are shot simply using their mobile devices and uploaded straight to *YouTube* using a variety of applications, which can do a pretty amazing job, in fact.

But if you trawl through the *YouTube* catalog you'll find that the quality of the videos does vary widely. In a way, that's the beauty and fun of *YouTube*: its sheer anarchic nature. And it would be pretty boring if all the videos were the same and all had the same production qualities with perfectly polished video and sound, all conforming to some arbitrary standard.

Now I'm not saying you too can't produce crazy, wacky videos if that's your style and it fits in with your particular niche. If such videos are engaging and fun for your viewers, then by all means go for it!

But for me, I tend to make informational or instructional videos and they need to have certain qualities in order to be effective. In short, they need to be clear, concise, easy to understand and provide information that's of value to the viewer.

And as part of this process you also need to remember to put in a bit of *yourself* into the videos. This can mean putting yourself in front of a camera and simply talking or simply narrating a screencast video.

What doesn't work so well is posting up a self-running PowerPoint presentation to a music soundtrack. It's simply not emotionally engaging to the viewer. I'm sure you know the kind of thing I mean - a presentation is whizzing past you to loud or simply inane music and you're left with a mainly stunned emotion at the end of it - if you even make it to the end before switching off!

People will start to turn away pretty quick with these types of videos and they simply won't come back. There's simply no level of trust built up between you and the viewer when you do it this way. The viewer will feel that you're not credible and may even feel insulted that you won't put yourself in front of them and show your personality in some way.

And this interaction is important.

The audience needs to know that they can trust you and like you and what you have to say. This is what keeps them coming back for more. And this is what will ultimately lead to more sales!

So whatever you do, follow this simple rule:

Tip: Use your own face, or at a bare minimum, your own voice in all of your videos.

Other points to note are:

- You don't need to be Mr. Magnetism when presenting your videos. I know I'm not! So don't try to be something you're not. So use your own personality. It may feel a little weird at first if you've never done it before, but the more you do it, the easier and more natural it will become.

- Speak clearly and concisely into the microphone. Many *YouTube* videos have very poor quality sound, and strangely poor sound is almost *more* distracting to me than poor quality video, particularly with screencast videos. It sounds such an obvious point I know but you really can lose visitors over it. (I have a list of microphones I recommend in the Appendix section to suit all budgets).

- If you're doing a screencast video remove all clutter and distractions from your desktop - so lose the 300 icons and the picture of a naked woman from your wallpaper! You should ideally have just a 'My Computer' icon at the top left and a pastel-colored screen, and that's it!

- Make sure there's no outside traffic noise, kids running around, or other distractions.

Prepare a detailed script and do a couple of run-throughs first. Remember, you have as many takes as you want!

Too many um's and ah's can be extremely distracting!

I've posted a script document on my website at:

http://www.onlyplacetogo.com/free-downloads,

which you're welcome to download and use. It's simply a numbered table with columns for completing what you're going to say and what actions you're going to take whilst saying them!

Tip: Keep your videos around 5-7 minutes long.

Try to keep your videos short, around 5-7 minutes, as audiences generally tend to lose concentration after then. If you have more to say, then split your videos into different parts. Google and *YouTube* love videos that form part of a series, as do your viewers and research has shown that it keeps them on your channel for longer. You can also cross-promote each video inside the videos themselves, as well as the descriptions.

I don't want to be too prescriptive here and stifle your creativity, but audiences can be very fickle and can be turned off by the silliest of things in your videos. So try to eliminate these obvious ones at least!

2 KEYWORD RESEARCH

Tip: Use valuable keywords

Like Google, when uploading videos to *YouTube*, you need to consider what keywords you're going to be targeting for that video.

It's no use simply posting a video to your *YouTube* channel and expecting visitors to flock to view it in their thousands, no matter how good you think the quality of your videos are.

Sure, many videos do go viral, but they are extremely few and far between so please don't rely on this method alone, unless you're in a highly unusual niche, or with one hell of a fantastic set of videos!

For the rest of us, we need to think about what our potential viewers will be typing into the search engines to find our videos, rather than simply relying on word of mouth!

And clever as it is, Google is not able to determine the exact content of our videos without keywords to guide it, so we need to give it a bit of a helping hand.

When you do use keywords, make them valuable keywords, phrases that people are actually typing into the search engines! More on this in next section.

Tip: Do not treat Google and YouTube the same!

Unlike Google, the rules are very much more relaxed with *YouTube* and they need to be treated as quite different animals.

I liken *YouTube* to how Google was 10-15 years ago; it's like the Hot Tub Time Machine of internet marketing!

Many of the strict algorithms that Google have imposed on their own search engine simply don't apply to *YouTube*; you have much more of a free rein. To *YouTube*, Panda and Penguin are simply cute animal videos!

People make the mistake of confusing Google and *YouTube* and will often tread a little too carefully when adding keywords in their titles, tags and descriptions for fear of getting penalized.

Yes, there are things you shouldn't do, (like simply repeating the same keywords over and over, and remember to keep them all closely relevant to your topic) but equally there are plenty of things you can do to put yourself way ahead of the competition.

You simply can't use too many keywords and, believe it or not the more keywords the merrier! This is all because the search engine needs as many clues as to what your content is about as it can get, unlike traditional websites where Google and the other search engines can determine what your site is about by simply crawling your text and links.

So you need to exploit this Achilles' Heel; very few people do! This is one of the big secrets to getting a ton of free traffic on *YouTube*. And choosing the right keywords is the major difference between both Google and *YouTube* putting you at the top or the bottom of the rankings.

Let's start by looking at your video Filename.

.

YOUR VIDEO FILENAME

OK, probably not the most crucial element, but we should start as we mean to go on. Although only a small factor in the whole scheme of things, it's thought that YouTube still uses your video file as one indicator of your actual video content. And it's all about the aggregation of marginal gains!

Not only that, but it keeps your video library organized if, later on down the line, when your videos start to number in the hundreds, you have no clue as to the contents of each one!

Use hyphens if possible in order to keep it all file names readable both by you and the search engines. So let's say your video is about aggressive hamsters, you might name your file: "when-hamsters-attack.mov".

To further stay organized, it's also good practice to keep each distinct video series in a separate folder on your PC. Makes it so much easier when referring back to them later, rather than bundling everything into a single folder.

OK, now on to a far more crucial matter - your Video Title.

YOUR TITLE

Your title is absolutely the first thing you need to think about once you've posted your video and so many people don't fully exploit this. When a potential viewer is trawling through a list of thumbnails, the title can be the clincher that can make or break the deal.

If their curiosity is piqued by a compelling title, your video has a much greater chance of being chosen from the masses.

Tip: Use as near to 60 words as you can in your title.

The title is important both from a search point of view also for relaying the content of the video to the user, so it needs to serve a dual purpose. As well as being a high-ranking keyword, ideally it also needs to emotionally draw the audience in to *want* to watch the video.

The easiest way to get the best keywords for your title is to head over to:

https://adwords.google.com/ko/KeywordPlanner/Home

If you haven't already (and I'm sure you have), create a Google Adwords account before doing this. If you use the keyword planner tool with a logged on Google Adwords account you will get many additional keyword ideas to use. Particularly useful in the next 2 sections*!*

OK, let's say I was going to post a video on the subject of ranking in *YouTube*. My first most obvious choice might be: *"How to Rank in YouTube"*.

Tip: Put the phrase you want to rank for at the beginning of the Title.

Let's see the Adwords Keyword Suggestion result for this:

Your product or service

how to rank in youtube

Ad group ideas	Keyword ideas		
Search Terms		Avg. monthly searches [?]	Competition [?]
how to rank in youtube		20	Low

OK not great, as you can see, there are only 20 users searching for this phrase each month.

But hang on, according to Google, *YouTube* reads the first 55-60 characters of the title and I've only used 22 characters. And as I said previously, *YouTube* actually *WANTS* you to use this allowance. Remember, it wants as many clues as it can get its hand on as to the true content of your videos.

Plus I now need to appeal to the audience's emotions. Let's improve on this title. Going back to my keyword results, I see just the thing:

Search Terms	Avg. monthly searches	Competition
how to get more views on youtube	5,400	Medium

So my headline Title is now *"How to get more views on YouTube: How to get rank in YouTube!"*. Much better.

Hmm, suspiciously similar to my Amazon book title!

I've used pretty much all of my allowance and fitted two very nice high value key phrases into the mix. I've also helped *YouTube* to identify the content of my video and thrown in a bit of emotion into the mix as well - amazing what you can squeeze into a single *YouTube* Title!

We'll refer to this as your *headline key phrase*, but as you can see we've sneaked in 2 key phrases here, so I now have 2 headline key phrases for the price of one! You'll use these in the next sections too. Try also to think of the title in the same way as a newspaper editor would and treat it: like an attention-grabbing headline. Remember, this will be seen by your potential audience as well as the search engines and they make their decision to click or not, based on your Title, so make it compelling.

Tip: Get 2 headline key phrases in your title and make it an 'emotional' headline.

Remember to keep the headline closely relevant to the content - if you don't you'll find your bounce rate will increase i.e. viewers will click away from your video quickly, since the content simply won't be exactly what the audience is looking for. Google has certain key indicators it looks for when ranking your videos and bounce rate is one of them.

But we've only just started!

OK, now let's move on to the description.

YOUR DESCRIPTION

Your Description, like your Title, is read by your potential visitors, often whilst watching your videos, so this also needs to serve a dual purpose:

- it needs to have plenty of good valuable key phrases for YouTube and the other search engines, and

- it needs to be interesting, informative and emotionally engaging to your audience.

Tip: Use your full description allowance.

Did you know how many words you are permitted to use in your description? Well very few people do.

In fact, you're allowed 5,000 characters! That's an awful lot of content and probably equates to around 700-800 words, the same as a typical WordPress post.

In fact, *YouTube* actually states in its search guidelines that it actually rewards longer Descriptions, so please don't hold back!

It may seem like a chore to write such a long Description but believe me it will be worth it. After all, this video may be earning you an income for many years to come with no additional work required, so doesn't it pay to get to spend the time crafting a good one?

So in my case I would compile a whole list of keywords using the Adwords Keyword Planner Tool, including the headline keyphrases from my title and work them all into the description.

However, it's also important to keep the description looking natural and to only use the phrases where it feels right to do so. It must not detract from the readability of the article. The article must make sense!

It's also important not to keep repeating the same keywords over and over and this will more than likely be penalized, so mix them up. In my case, I would try to work in phrases like "how to get more views in *YouTube*", or "increase *YouTube* views". You can afford to choose more 'low-hanging fruit' keywords in the description i.e. those with lower search results, unlike the Title, where you want a nice big, juicy, valuable key phrase or two. These are known a 'long-tail keywords' and the great thing about these is that they have relatively low competition compared to your headline key phrases. So whilst they may not have as many people searching for them, you have an extremely good chance of ranking highly for them!

Tip: Try to have one of your headline keyphrases in the first and last sentence of your description

Also, make sure you choose relevant keyphrases; they must stay on-topic or again or you may well be penalized by *YouTube*.

In fact, a long, well-crafted, interesting and emotionally engaging description has another of those 'double-whammy' effects I talked about earlier: not only does it rank you higher in the search results, it also keeps the users on your channel for longer while they read it, which *YouTube* by the way will also take note of (a decreased bounce rate)!

But the main reason for using your full allowance is to increase the odds of a visitor finding you using one of the keyphrases you have worked into your article. And by writing more, you're able to sneak these in more readily without it looking spammy or false to either the reader or the search engine.

So remember, use all 5,000 characters. Yes, every last one!

And finally and this is a very important thing that people miss:

Tip: Put a link to the video itself at the end of the Description.

This is very important. Why? Well, think about it - if someone shares your video on say, a social bookmarking site, inside the description itself is a direct link back to your own video. Google will crawl this and it will add an awful lot of weight to your videos. Not to mention the countless viewers clicking back to your *YouTube* channel from these links!

USING TAGS

Here we come to perhaps the most under-used and perhaps least understood area, *Tags.*

Tip: use at least 10 Tags, and include your headline keyphrases in them.

Although your visitors don't actually see them, *YouTube* does and it laps them up since it provides another big clue as to how they should categorize and rank your videos. However, so few people take full advantage of them. They simply throw in a couple of random barely related words, usually suggested by *YouTube* and they're done! If you do this, your missing out on a whole load of traffic since *YouTube* places a great deal of importance to Tags after the Title and Description.

You already have your keywords from your Title and Description, so you simply need to place them in here too, perhaps with slight variations.

Make sure you put quotation marks around your most important phrases. So for instance, I might have:

"How to Rank in YouTube"

"How to get more views on YouTube"

"How to increase subscribers on YouTube"

"How to get more viewers to your YouTube channel"

And so on. Remember to put your best key phrases first.

You can have as many tags as you think are appropriate, but I would say you need to use at least 10. By having some phrases without quotations, you are increasing your chances of being found where users are changing the order of the words in the phrase. And by having quotations around some, you also ensure you rank highly for that exact key phrase too. So mix and match as appropriate.

Don't simply choose single words like "*YouTube*" or "views" (which *YouTube* will often unhelpfully suggest!) as these are fairly meaningless and far to general and really won't bring in any more significant traffic, and even if it did, it's unlikely it would be very targeted traffic, which after all is what we are after.

We don't want views just for the hell of it, or from people who will immediately turn off; we want visitors that are actually going to watch our video and be converted to customers, don't we?

And again, as with the Title and Description, don't simply repeat the keyphrases over and over and remember to keep them all firmly on-topic. The Google Adwords Keyword Planner tool will give you more than enough suggestions to use when logged in to your Adwords account.

3 ENGAGING YOUR VIEWERS

OK, so you've got your viewers to your video. Now what?

What's your ultimate goal for this video? If you're doing this as way of gaining an income from it, you may wish to monetize the site by simply placing a Google Ad at the beginning of the video.

You do this by simply signing up for a Google Analytics account and then clicking the *Monetization* option on your video whilst in *Edit* mode:

| Basic info | **Monetisation** | Advanced settings |

☑ **Monetise with Ads**

Ad Formats

☑ Overlay in-video ads
☑ TrueView in-stream ads
☐ This video contains a paid product placement

Display ads are shown by default.

Syndication

● Everywhere
  make this video available on all platforms

○ Monetised platforms
  make this video available only on monetised platforms

In many cases, you'll want to send them to a *funnel* site, i.e. a page on your own website that will 'close the deal'. This might involve asking them to sign up to your newsletter in return for a free report, perhaps, completing an enquiry form where you then contact them about your products, or simply sending them to a related product via an affiliate link.

Either way, you need to find a way to get the user to 'make themselves at home' on your channel, to build up that all-important trust level and to put them in that buying frame of mind.

There are a couple of features in *YouTube* that can greatly assist in this process, the *Annotation* and the *Call-to-Action Overlay*.

Let's look at Annotations first.

USING ANNOTATIONS

What are Annotations?

Annotations are basically notes you can lay on top of your videos add anywhere to the timeline of your videos to provide additional information.

Tip: Make use of Annotations!

I would recommend using these as a call to action to your audience, asking them to do certain things at different parts of the video. For instance, I will often add an Annotation during the video to ask for a 'Thumbs Up' of my video. I've noticed that the audience often respond positively and when I do ask my Likes actually increase.

To find them, simply click on the Edit button for your video and you'll find the Annotations tab above your video.

You can add as many Annotations as you like and then simply select where on the timeline you want to appear and for how long. Simply drag the bar to where you'd like it to appear.

Although you can use Annotations as labels to provide information in your videos, I tend to find them more useful as 'calls to action'. Your video software is more than capable of making its own 'in-video' labels so it just seems a waste to use them just for this purpose alone!

If you're short of comments and would like to get some more, just change your Annotation to read: "Please comment below if you Like this video!". This can be very useful if you ever receive a bad comment, which can sometime snowball into further bad comments. Once you add these annotations, it tends to get the community on your side and they end up defending your video. Annotations can really be that powerful.

If this video is part of a series, then use the Annotation to draw their attention to your related videos.

It's really amazing what you can achieve simply by asking using Annotations - sometimes the audience simply needs a little nudge to help you out!

Research has found that having the Annotations 'pop up' during the video gets the best results, rather than simply having the Annotation permanently stuck there for the whole length of the video. So you might want it to pop up in the middle and one later on towards the end of your videos.

You can even use the Analytics feature in *YouTube* to decide the optimum pop-up time for these messages, based on the average viewing time of your video so you grab them before they switch off! To do this, within your *YouTube* Dashboard, go to 'Analytics'. In here click on 'Audience Retention'.

HOW TO RANK IN YOUTUBE

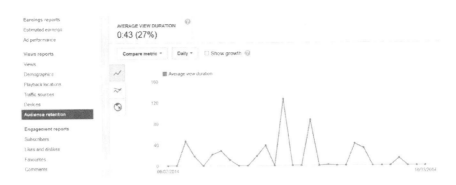

MAKING YOUR VIDEOS 'CLICKABLE'

A very powerful and little known feature exists in YouTube, known as the 'Call-to-Action Overlay'. This effectively allows you to place a clickable link at the bottom of your videos, which viewers can click on and go to wherever you send them.

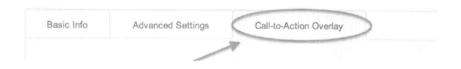

The problem is, the Call-to-Action Overlay link only shows up once you are running a Campaign. But fear not, I have a workaround that won't cost you a penny!

First, if you don't already have once, set up an Adwords account with Google by visiting https://adwords.google.com. Use the same account you are signed into in *YouTube*.

Now create a new Campaign, and make sure you choose 'Online Video'.

Fill in the various sections (ensuring you enter a low figure in the 'Budget' box, just in case you forget to pause the Campaign!), choose the video you wish to apply it to and then save the Campaign.

Now head back over to *YouTube*, Edit your video and hey Presto! you'll find that the Call-to-Action Overlay tab has now magically appeared in the tabs below your video!

Now go back to the Campaign and simply pause it! You can now add your own clickable overlays onto your videos, which appear at the bottom of your videos for the first 5 seconds of playing. You can use this to direct them to any URL you like and customize the text to your heart's content. This may be a sales page or simply a link to another related video.

Why *YouTube* haven't latched onto this loophole I can't say for sure but I suspect it's by design: they want to demonstrate the usefulness of this feature to you in the hope that you will eventually use it conjunction with a real Ad campaign!

I've had no troubles with it to date and the overlay tab continues to remain to this day on all my videos. Whether it will be withdrawn at some later date I honestly can't say, but while the loophole remains, you should use it.

The click-thru rates are definitely higher using overlays, rather than simply relying on your viewers to click on a hyperlink somewhere within your Description.

What you can't do is Monetize your videos AND have Call-to-Action Overlays. It's either one or the other. Personally I much prefer overlays as you can direct the user to a funnel page where you can continue to sell your wares.

With the monetization feature, a random ad is shown to the viewers and you may get a few pence if the user clicks on it before skipping the Ad after the 5 second limit is reached. This can be a real turn-off to the viewer, who simply wants to see your video and not be subjected to an unrelated advert prior to viewing it!

I strongly recommend you dive in and try these Call-to-Action Overlays as it can really help the 'stickiness' of your video channel, keeping your viewers on your Channel for longer.

Tip: Don't forget to pause those Campaigns!

'IN-VIDEO' CAPTIONS

One other area that many people overlook is the captions inside the videos themselves. It may surprise you to know that YouTube can read any captions inside your videos. So we may as well make use of them!

Tip: Put your Headline Keyphrase in the captions within your videos.

This may be in the form of a page at the beginning or end of your videos or as labels during play that you insert during the production process. *YouTube* does read these and they will undoubtedly help your rankings.

So make sure you put your headline keyphrases in here too. I will usually add an introductory screen to the beginning of my videos, which will include the main keyphrase. You can do this inside the video editors themselves, whether it's Microsoft Movie Maker or Camtasia Studio, etc.

This not only helps your *YouTube* ranking but also gives viewers a heads up as to exactly what this video is all about prior to watching, and if you have a compelling caption, make them even more likely to click on it. With *YouTube* you get a choice of 3 thumbnails to use so if you do have a catchy opening caption then make sure this is the thumbnail you choose.

I will also include something similar at the end of the video, along with any instructions for the viewer to follow, namely to visit whichever site for which I'm promoting that particular product.

Finally, remember to put your contact details and website address on this page too.

4 SUPERCHARGING YOUR TRAFFIC

OK so far we've looked at:

- What equipment you'll need;

- How to do your keyword research;

- How best to complete your Title, Tags and Descriptions for maximum impact;

- How to use Annotations in the most effective way;

- How to use Call-to-Action Overlays to make your videos clickable;

- Using in-video captions;

You're already way ahead of most of the competition already!

By following the above you've made your videos more discoverable, more enticing, your key phrases on-topic and have ensured your videos are engaging and are also cross-promoting each other effectively.

This will go a really long way to addressing and covering off most of the major factors that *YouTube* considers when ranking your video, namely:

- How many times the video is watched over a period of time;

- How much feedback you're receiving in the comments section;

- How long people spend watching your video(s);

- How many times it's been shared on other user's playlists;

- How many positive reviews it gets;

- How often it's been shared on other blogs/social bookmarking site.

Which brings us on to the next part which is all about taking these solid foundations you've just built to the next level - by getting those all-important backlinks to your videos.

BEGIN CLOSE TO HOME

One easy way to get your very first comments and reviews is to use your friends and family!

I find the best way is to create my own email distribution list of all my friends and family members and then send out an email with a link to my video inviting them to check it out.

And in the email you simply nudge them to rate it (kindly!) and to provide comments (the longer the better).

Just as with Amazon, your audience likes to see social proof, and although it's not going to skyrocket your view count, it certainly makes your videos more credible and users more likely to watch them and to even review them too.

As with reviews, video commenting is also very useful. But adding comments is a bit like putting your hand up in class: no-one likes to be the first one to do it!

But, armed with your handful of comments, others will feel much more comfortable adding their own.

Just request that if your friends and family do have anything negative to say about your videos, it's probably best to email you directly, rather than posting a comment about it!

On the other hand, some more controversial comments can actually have the effect of starting a discussion on your video, drawing more people in; but probably best they run it past you first!

Once done, this will 'prime' your video ready for the big wide world, where it can start competing with the big guys!

GETTING BACKLINKS

Another big factor that Google uses when deciding how to rank your videos is the number, quality and relevance of incoming links to your videos.

Now there's a lot of things you can do to get backlinks to your videos, including posting on related forums and blog posts as well as *Facebook*, *Twitter*, Social Bookmarking sites like *Digg* and *Delicious* and Article Directories like *Squidoo*, *Hubpages* and *Ezinearticles*.

We saw in the description section how, by putting a link back to your video in your Description, you can gain an additional ranking benefit when anyone shares one of your videos. Well that's just the start.

You basically use exactly the same strategies as you would use to gain backlinks to your own website. This is a huge topic in itself and outside the scope of this book. However, I cover this in much more detail in my first book, How to Rank in Google: SEO Strategies post Panda and Penguin. I strongly encourage you to follow the strategies in this book as there is a big overlap and many of the approaches you use here will help with your video rankings in exactly the same way.

Each and every additional backlink to your video will raise its rankings that little bit higher each time so try to make it part of your daily task to get at least 1 additional backlink to your video.

This may be a mention on your Twitter or Facebook account, or a post on a related forum together with your video link. But remember, when posting on forums not to simply stick up your link, as you may get short shrift from the moderator. So provide good quality information that adds value, especially for the first few posts. Then, when you feel it's time, you might helpfully suggest your video in response to a certain 'on-topic' request.

Tip: Ensure you have a targeted backlink from your website to your YouTube video

One trick that many overlook when getting backlinks to their own site, is a link from their very own blog! Remember, your blog is fully 'on-topic' and is a great place to start! People will often post their *YouTube* videos on their own site, but they then forget to post a link back to their own video anywhere else on their site using their headline keyphrases!

If you aren't doing this, you're missing out on a lot of potential free traffic! One of my videos was floundering on around page 9 of Google, but soon after putting a targeted backlink to that video (using the exact headline keyphrase), I was on page 1 within a couple of weeks!

So once you've posted up your video your strategy should be to do the following:

- Tweet about it (with a link back to it using one of your headline keyphrases);

- Post something on Facebook about it (with a link back to it using one of your headline keyphrases);

- Write about it on Google+ (with a link back to it using one of your headline keyphrases!);

- Write about it on at least 3 Article Directories - Squidoo,

Ezinearticles, etc (with a link back , etc.!);

- Post a link to it on at least 3 Social Bookmarking sites - Digg, Delicious, etc (with a link back, etc!);

- Start posting on related forums about it, with occasional links back to your video, using, you guessed it, one of your headline keyphrases!

You can mix up your headline keyphrase backlinks but have at least 10 with exact match keyphrases that you want to rank for to keep this firmly in the mind of Google et al when deciding your ranking position for these keyphrases.

OUTSOURCING

It can sometimes be useful to use outsourcers to promote your products or even to produce the videos for you.

In an ideal world you would produce your own video reviews in front of camera or via a screencast and talk about your own products. This is by far the most credible way to promote your products. Nothing shouts credibility like you promoting your own products.

However, there are some circumstances where you may not want to do this.

For instance, you may not simply be comfortable being in front of camera, or maybe you're involved in a number of different niches and you don't want to lose your credibility in one particular niche by promoting products in another. I have used outsourcers to produce video reviews of my kindle books where I'm writing under a different pen name. If you are using them for reviews you don't need to go overboard on these - 3 or 4 video reviews per product is more than enough.

You can use exactly the same strategies in this book on these videos as you would do on your own videos.

One website in particular, *Fiverr.com* is very useful for doing this and for $5 you can actually get quite a decent video produced. Many of these outsourcers have been using *YouTube* for many years and are seasoned professionals with all the latest equipment and are often great performers in front of camera. For an additional $5 - $15 you can get extra features like longer length videos or additional production features such as a professional music soundtrack to go along with the narration.

The two main advantages of this method are:

- You can produce lots of videos very quickly;
- You don't need to invest in any equipment.

Once posted, you simply use the techniques in this book to rank for them!

Although not obligatory, outsourced videos can still do a great job of driving traffic and increasing sales and can be another valuable weapon in your armory!

Quite another way to use outsourcing, which I do recommend, is to get more views and to assist you in your link-building strategies, coming up next...

GETTING MORE VIEWS

OK, we all know that as part of your SEO strategy, a big no-no is to pay for 'fake' views. What I'm referring to here is the kind of views that are *automated.*

There are a number of products out there that do exactly that, where you can simply type in the URL of your video and a computer program, using a variety of accounts, will literally 'view' your videos for you, supposedly boosting your link-juice. This may have worked in the past, but not anymore. I strongly advise against using this tactic as it could not only seriously harm your rankings, but could get your account banned into the bargain!

What I'm talking about here are real views (well let's call them 'human views'). And there are plenty of outsourcing sites that will view your videos for you.

Currently the best outsourcing sites for doing this are:

- Microworkers (www.microworkers.com);

- Amazon Mechanical Turk (www.mturk.com);

- oDesk (www.odesk.com);

- Fiverr (www.fiverr.com).

You simply post your job and select your candidate(s) and off they'll go, doing your bidding! But remember, *YouTube* wants to see that people are staying to watch your videos so make sure that whoever you chose watches at least 50% of its length.

If done right, you'll see a noticeable effect on your rankings using this tactic, and increasingly *YouTube* holds a great deal of store in both the number of views of your videos, along with the number comments. But beware of the more 'spammy' services, and make sure that you thoroughly check out real reviews of whoever you plan to use first.

But isn't outsourcing risky?

As with all outsourcing strategies, they always carry some element of risk. So my advice here is: slowly, slowly, catchy monkey - don't overdo it and make it look as natural as possible. And try to get a good balance of views, reviews and comments. If *YouTube* suddenly see that you have no views one day and 5,000 the next, along with zero comments or reviews, then you'd expect them to be suspicious. It's for this reason that I avoid the dedicated *YouTube* viewing services; I also believe that *YouTube* have their cards marked since they're using many of the same accounts for all of their customers and Google are now pretty good at pattern-matching!

This is a reason I love the crowd-sourcing sites like *Amazon Mechanical Turk* and *MicroWorkers*, which spread the workload (and the risk) amongst many disparate people!

But let's put things into perspective here with outsourcing: most banning by *YouTube* is done to people offering:

- less than savory products,

- overly promotional content, or

- offensive material.

You're simply trying to lift your head slightly above the massing crowd of your competitors, without spending every waking moment of your life link-building yourself!

PAD LINKS

For some people, this is a slightly contentious one, but currently it's also a very well-used strategy by many in the know!

What is a PAD file?

PAD files (Portable Application Description) were designed to be used by the authors and publishers in the shareware software community as a standardized way of cataloguing their software into types and genres, so that users could find their software easily on the internet.

A PAD file contains the software title, descriptions and specifications of the software.

However, it's now been increasingly exploited by other communities as a way of promoting videos, audio files, books, even backlinks to their own websites! So why not jump on the bandwagon?

You can create a PAD file that simply contains a title, description and link back to your video and then submit this to the hundreds of PAD software sharing sites around the internet; each one giving you a very nice backlink.

PAD files still currently fly fairly low under the radar of *YouTube*, so it can be a very useful way of getting a good selection of backlinks, especially if you're linking back to a good 'How-to' or review video - you're simply reaching out and providing your audience with good, solid, useful information - now how can that be a bad thing?

Creating and distributing PAD files

Although you're more than welcome to, I really wouldn't advise wasting lots of time creating one of these files, nor of submitting them manually. Much better to outsource both tasks!

The best outsourcing site to use, as ever, is *Fiverr*. You simply use one gig to get your PAD file created and another to distribute it!

Just drop me line if you'd like to know which gigs I use to get my PAD files created and distributed.

SOCIAL BOOKMARKING

Another task that lends itself extremely well to outsourcing is Social Bookmarking. After all, the result is exactly the same as if you do it yourself; the only difference being you'll still have a life you can call your own!

What is Social Bookmarking?

Social Bookmarking is basically the act of going out into the big wide internet world and shouting to everyone that you have something you'd like to share with them, by *bookmarking* or *tagging* a site.

Social Bookmarking sites aggregate everything that's going on in the internet world, whether it's a post on a blog, a Tweet, or a video that someone wants to share with the world.

These sites don't care too much who tags them or even what is bookmarked and for this reason, adding a bookmark to a site has very little impact on your overall rankings or views. However, outsourcers are able to bookmark your link to hundreds of social bookmarking sites at once! Try doing this yourself manually and your life will no longer be your own!

With your link existing on 1,000 social bookmarking sites, things begin to get more interesting!

This one's an easy win and for 5 bucks it really is a no-brainer!

5 REPURPOSING YOUR VIDEOS

One really powerful way of promoting your message is to repurpose your content.

Repurposing is the act of re-releasing the same content in a variety of formats. After all, you've already spent valuable time putting together all the material for your video, so why not make the most of it and maximize its potential?

The best marketers realize the power of repurposing. Take Disney, for instance. They'll often take ideas from fairy tales (copyright free by the way), and produce a movie from the original story. They'll then adapt the premise of the original movie to branch into other movies and sequels. Along the way, from each of these movies they'll create books, audio books, spin-off cartoon series, toys, merchandise, etc, etc...!

So why not take the Disney approach and turn your own video content into:

- an audio book?

- a Podcast?

- a report that you can sell or that can go on your blog?

- an eBook?

- a video series that people can buy either on DVD or via download?

Many of the content-sharing sites have a really high Page Rank, so provide you with very valuable backlinks.

Not only that but you can also re-issue your video to other video-sharing sites. This is where we'll start...

YOUTUBE IS NOT THE ONLY FRUIT

Although *YouTube* has the lion's share when it comes to video sharing, there is still a very sizeable audience sector present at a number of other sites.

Currently the best of these are:

- Vimeo (www.vimeo.com);
- Revver (www.revver.com);
- Metacafe (www.metacafe.com);
- Dailymotion (www.dailymotion.com);
- Viddler (www.viddler.com).

The advantage of publishing your videos to these sharing sites are twofold:

It obviously puts more eyes on your videos, but just as importantly,

It allows you to link back from the videos on these sites back to your *YouTube* channel - think of each of them as very valuable backlinks.

You may also be linking to a back-end product or maybe your own blog/sales funnel, in which case you can do this too, by either placing a link in the description boxes or within the video content itself (or both!).

And don't forget to post your videos on your blog, *Facebook* and *Myspace*, *WhatsApp*, *Path* and all your other social media accounts - each one is a very useful backlink.

Think of each additional posting as an extra lottery ticket, each one increasing your chances of getting seen by your audience.

REPURPOSING RITUAL

OK, so you've put your videos on all the main video-sharing sites and shared it on your social media accounts, now what?

Well you need to start thinking outside the box a little - you have all this content that's crying out to be published in a variety on new formats!

There's a whole plethora of sharing sites out there, capable of displaying your content in a variety of formats; and the content has already been created with very little additional 'translation' work from you!

Think about how you can:

1. Produce an audiobook from your video series (www.audible.com)

2. Produce a podcast series from your videos at:

    - Podbean (www.podbean.com)

    - Podomatic (www.podomatic.com)

    - iTunes (www.apple.com/uk/itunes/podcasts/specs.html)

3. Create an Infographic of your video and post on sharing sites such as:

   - Visual.ly (http://visual.ly/)

   - Daily Infographic (www.dailyinfographic.com)

   - Pinterest (www.pinterest.com)

Infographics are notoriously difficult to create, but there are experts out there on Fiverr and oDesk who are seasoned experts on this process and can create stunning infographics with minimal briefing.

4. Create a video training series and sell either on your own site or via a third party such as CreateSpace or *Mindbites*.

5. Create a PDF 'cheat sheet' of your content with links back to your video/product/blog/sales funnel. People love freebies!

6. Create an eBook on Amazon Kindle (kdp.amazon.com), or as a physical book (www.createspace.com).

7. How about producing your content in a variety of languages, using outsourcing?

Now I'm not saying you need to do ALL of the above; certain content lends itself better to different kinds of repurposing and some formats may not be applicable.

However, don't simply dismiss an idea simply because you've never done it this way before. Let's get creative with this content and fully realize its full potential!

Remember, each new repurposing gives your videos more exposure, and many of the sites you'll be publishing to are extremely high Page Rank sites, which means they are providing you with highly valuable backlinks and raising your online profile.

SUMMARY

As you can see, to rank high in *YouTube* involves a many-pronged approach. But equally many of the things you need to do are really pretty straightforward and most of the techniques take up very little time. Once you make them part of your routine, then it just gets easier and easier.

You need to realize that a few *You-Tubers* are following some of these strategies but only a very small number are following *all* of them and that's where you can leapfrog your competition and have that traffic flooding in.

So pick just one of your videos today, work through each of the sections, see where they may be falling short and correct them, one by one. I guarantee that you'll see noticeable results before long if you use the strategies in this book.

Ensure throughout that your content is of good quality and is providing value and giving people what they want.

Ad Campaigns

I haven't touched on using paid traffic and find that in the niches I am in I simply haven't required it. However, if you can afford it then I see no problem in using Ad Campaigns. I just believe that in most niches that you can still get a great deal of traffic without needing to pay for it! When your business takes off however, then paid traffic can indeed take you to even greater levels if done right.

Affiliate Links

A quick word on using affiliate links - don't use them! And don't even put them as watermarks inside your videos. If you link directly to an affiliate site using a masked link, you could just get all your videos removed. So always send your viewers to a funnel site where you can then direct them to your recommended product or service.

And build up your *YouTube* channel to keep your viewers interested, cross-promoting each of them inside your other videos. If you only have one solitary video up there, you may struggle!

You could even ask them to subscribe to your channel using your Annotations. It's all about generating a buzz around your sites so use your website, *Twitter*, *Facebook* and the rest to keep generating this interest. Get on those forums related to your niche and get commenting!

Please feel free to email me if you have any questions at james@onlyplacetogo.com.

You can also find me on *Twitter* and *Facebook*.

Finally, if you want help with ranking on Google as well, you may be interested in my first book in the series, and you can even request to join my Facebook Group: *How to Rank in Google*. All I ask in return is an honest review of my book on Amazon!

I sincerely hope you've found this book useful and I wish you the best of luck with all your endeavors. Please send me your success stories!

All the very best,

James Green

APPENDIX - EQUIPMENT AND RESOURCES

The following are the equipment I use or have used. I'm in no way being prescriptive here - use what you are comfortable with and works for you.

Software:

Camtasia Studio (www.techsmith.com/camtasia.html) - quite expensive but well worth it if you plan to produce lots of videos. It's a screencast one-stop shop and the market leader.

Hardware:

Samson C01UCW Studio USB Microphone - a great mid-range USB microphone that provides great sound quality.

Blue Microphones Yeti USB Microphone - a simply stunning condenser microphone that gives crystal-clear vocals.

The following are alternatives if you want to dip your toe in the water to begin with. You can still produce great videos with them and, as I always say, it's the quality of the content that's the most important thing.

Alternative Software:

Camstudio (camstudio.org) - free open source software that will produce pretty decent screencasts.

Microsoft Movie Maker - great for editing your Camstudio videos - and it's free with Windows 7.

Audacity (audacity.sourceforge.net) - great for editing sound clips and music intros for your videos. Again, free open-source software.

Snagit (http://www.techsmith.com/snagit.html) - less expensive than Camtasia but a surprisingly full-featured screencast software.

Zoomit - a free utility that allows you to zoom in to an area of your screen as well as make simple live annotations during a presentation.

Alternative Hardware:

Trust Starzz Microphone - a very inexpensive microphone which produces surprisingly high quality results. Even comes with its own stand. I used to have this model and it served me very well in the past.

USB mics are always preferable, but this mic is simply a line-in model with a 3.5mm jack and is still more than acceptable until you're ready to move to the next level.

Useful Resources:

Google Keyword Tool

YouTube Keyword Tool

How to Rank in Google Book - My first book in the 'How to Rank in' series - many of the strategies in this book will also help boost your video rankings.

OTHER BOOKS IN THIS SERIES

If you enjoyed this book, then you might like to check out the other books in the "How to Rank in..." series, also available on Amazon:

How to Rank in Google SEO Strategies post Panda and Penguin,

and

How to Rank on Amazon: How to Self-Publish on Amazon Kindle Profitably

Made in the USA
San Bernardino, CA
06 August 2014